15(

MW01288727

Self-Care Activities

Christine Scott-Hudson

Dedication

This book is dedicated to my wonderful husband. Thank you for giving me so much support for over twenty years! You are my best friend. I love you.

About The Author

Christine Scott-Hudson is a Licensed Marriage and Family Therapist, Registered Clinical Art Therapist, Certified Somatic Therapist, Creative Wellness Expert, and is the owner of Create Your Life Studio. www.createyourlifestudio.com. She lives in beautiful Santa Barbara, California with her hilarious husband and their two darling dogs.

Christine Scott-Hudson, MA MFT ATR

LicensedPsychotherapist and Owner of @createyourlifestudio

www.createyourlifestudio.com

Self-care isn't selfish. Self-care is sacred. Self-care is necessary.

During the holidays, self-care is needed more than ever!

1.   Slow down.

2.   Sing Christmas Carols loudly in the car.

3.   Send secret holiday cards to those who need some good cheer.

4.   Bake something delicious and seasonal. Take some over to share with your elderly neighbors.

5.   Observe the family drama, but don't engage.

6.   Hang fairy lights in the kids' bedrooms.

7.   Bundle up and then go for a walk with family members after dinner.

8.   Skip Black Friday.

9. Shop Small Business Saturday. Meet a friend for PSL before you check our all of the cool, local artisan crafts!

10. Put some cute, warm, and toasty flannel sheets on your bed, on the kids' beds, and/or on the guest bed.

11. Remember that imperfect hostessing is ok! Have a few friends over, but not for a technical "party. "

12. Meet friends for pancakes in your holiday pajamas!

13. Have a spa night...face masks, deep condition your hair, manis, pedis-the works! Do funny beauty routines like charcoal tooth powder, soft feet peels, or Korean animal-face beauty masks. Listen to holiday music while you spa, and catch up with your girls, or snuggle in and listen to podcasts and make it an introvert spa night.

14. Hug yourself while you put on holiday scented lotion. Put

holiday scented lotion on your kids' backs for a sensory, soothing experience.

15.   Choose a holiday symbol to serve as your mindful pause reminder! Deep breathe every time you see a Santa, a Snowman, a Menorah, a reindeer, or a Star.

16.   Videotape an ordinary morning with your loveys. Videotape some holiday togetherness with your man, your partner, your kid, your parents, your grandparents, your siblings, your kitties, your dog, yourself. Everything could change in an instant. Savor the moment. Appreciate them now.

17.   Watch Elf.

18.   Watch old black and white holiday classics. The Shop around the Corner, White Christmas, etc.

19.   Watch the sun come up in the morning. Brew some good-smelling holiday coffee and savor the beauty.

20.   Settle in for some adult coloring.

21.   Don't overspend. Spend half as much money and twice as much time on your loved ones.

22.   Watch When Harry Met Sally.

23.   Listen to old records.

24.   Give each kid $5 to blow at a dollar store.

25.   Try a new cafe in a different part of town, instead of heading to your tried & true spot. A little novelty is good for you!

26.   Make handmade gifts. Watch a YouTube video with some kids, learn how to bake, sew, paint, craft, or knit a holiday gift.

27. Try a new holiday recipe, but not on a big night!

28. Take some family photos. They don't have to be perfect, but make sure mom is in them! Moms-get in the family photo! Make sure you are in the picture!

29. Open up the windows and air out the house.

30. Take deep breaths.

31. Make some festive Christmas punch.

32. De-stress by watching a soothing ASMR video on YouTube. Gentle Whispering is my favorite, she's so soothing, safe, and predictable.

33. Make faces on the plates out of the kids' breakfast foods-Santa, elf, reindeer, or snowman.

34. Let the kids do your holiday makeup. Take pictures.

35. Take a candlelight bath and use your favorite holiday smelling essential oils or bath bombs. Let your holiday troubles melt away!

36. Get a new book and read it in bed!

37. Watch a fireplace YouTube video.

38. Apologize.

39. Forgive.

40. Write out your hopes for the New Year.

41. Let it go.

42. Get a change of scenery-go for a drive or take a bus to another part of town. Check out the holiday displays, decorations, and lights.

43. Bring some holiday flowers, like poinsettias, to someone who is going through a lonely time. Write a card, too, to let them know how much they mean to you.

44. Get a massage!

45. Make a big pot of soup. Eat it with bread and butter.

46. Rock some super-kitschy holiday statement jewelry! Christmas light bulb earrings? Reindeer brooch? Menorah pin?

47. Start your morning out right and meditate or journal by candlelight.

48. Clear one small space and make a little altar.

49.   Light a fire in the fireplace or in a fire pit safely.

50.   Build a bonfire and invite some friends, new and old, over to hang out.

51.   Watch a YouTube video with some kids, learn how to bake, sew, paint, craft, or knit a holiday gift.

52.   Add Bailey's or Butterscotch Schnapps to your after-dinner coffee and play cards with your siblings and their partners.

53.   Put your smart phones away every evening of your children's holiday break. Let yourself be completely present, engaged, and in the moment.

54.   Go to bed an hour or two earlier! Rest up, buttercup.

55.   Build yourself, your partner, or your kids a super cozy and delightful little Hygge nook, somewhere in your

house. Set up an indoor tent, make a blanket fort, and put out all the fluffiest pillows & blankets to make a special spot for you to unwind, be quiet, and be calm.

56. Engage in a winter activity you used to love as a child, such as ice-skating, cross country skiing, building a snowman, making snow angels (or sand angels!)

57. Make a homemade gift for someone with your own two hands. You could make a picture frame, a pan of brownies, some fudge, a snow globe, a scarf, or an ornament.

58. Your crockpot is your bff during the busy holidays! Look on Pinterest for some delicious slow cooker comfort food recipes. Make a hearty chili or a nourishing stew. Make it easier on yourself!

59. Do quiet yoga, stretching, or dancing alone, by candlelight.

60. Do yoga, stretching, or dancing to holiday music. I really love George Winston's December.

61. Go for an entire weekend with your family unplugged from TV.

62. Bring the sights and smells of the great outdoors in. Bring in some holly berries, birch sticks, Rosemary, oranges, pinecones, greenery, etc.

63. Simmer a pot of oranges, cinnamon, and cloves on the stovetop.

64. Make holiday pomanders out of oranges and cloves. You can show children how to make these sensorial, wonderful smelling gifts.

65. Hygge up your holiday look! Wear a gorgeous holiday sweater, pull on some comfy leggings, wear a cute Pom Pom winter hat, wear some fashionable winter boots, and throw on a gorgeous scarf. Or, wear some festive

sparkle! Work it!

66.   Make a list of your year's highlights. Have the kids write theirs, too. Share them aloud at the dinner table.

67.   Listen to classical music to soothe your weary soul.

68.   Go outside on the porch, patio, or beach at night. Bundle up and look at the snow, the stars, the decorations, the trees, or the lights.

69.   Get some gorgeous new slippers. Enjoy the luxury.

70.   Place holiday flowers on the graves of loved ones who have passed away.

71.   Let the kids pick a recipe to try. Cook together as a family while you listen to holiday music.

72. Write a loving letter or a handmade Christmas card to one, a few, or several people who are dear to you.

73. Wear lotion, facial moisturizer, and chapstick.

74. Savor some chocolate. Don't share.

75. Savor some chocolate. Share.

76. Plan a movie night in with popcorn. Watch Mr. Bean's Holiday with the kids. Laugh!

77. Listen to a holiday podcast or to your favorite author read a holiday story on YouTube. Enjoy a classic, like "A Christmas Carol," or listen to a more modern story. "Holidays On Ice" by David Sedaris is a holiday fave.

78. Use the envelope system to stay on budget.

79. Engage your five senses: taste, sight, sound, touch, and smell. Notice what you can experience through the lens of your five senses. Help a child experience the holidays through their five senses, as well.

80. Call a family member and tell them that you love them.

81. Book one whole day of nothing, a day all to yourself over the holidays! Give yourself some room to breathe!

82. Watch an old holiday cartoon on YouTube.

83. Draw your family. Have the kids draw the family, too. Write one thing you appreciate about each person.

84. Get a little sun. Bundle up and get outside. Nature is medicine.

85. Start your day off with quiet reflection. Sip some holiday tea or coffee, light a candle, and write in your journal.

86. Offer to run to the store to get a few moments to yourself.

87. Respect your budget.

88. Let the kids interview their grandparents on video.

89. Put out a beautiful poinsettia, a vase full of flowers, or set a place at the table to honor your loved ones who have passed.

90. Be intentional.

91. Keep it simple.

92. Meditate.

93. Light some candles.

94.   Only decorate with your most favorite decorations this year.

95.   Have the kids draw what they want every year. Hold on to these keepsakes!

96.   Memorize a poem to be read on New Year's Day. Make it an annual tradition.

97.   Practice your holiday affirmations in the mirror. Shauna Niequist's "Present over perfect" is a great one to try! Another holiday affirmation is "All is well."

98.   Have a device-free evening. Play board games with the family. Sorry, Trouble, Monopoly, Clue, and Candy Land are all classic board games to enjoy.

99.   Drink some chai, chocolate chai, gingerbread, peppermint, or sugarplum tea. Drink it slowly and

mindfully.

100. If you are a highly sensitive person, avoid the center of the action. Avoid loud guests. Avoid the center of the room. Play with the animals, stay to the perimeters, or help out in the kitchen.

101. Watch free (and cheesy) Christmas TV Programming on TBS, Lifetime, The Hallmark Channel, etc. Indulge in the sap!

102. Treat yourself to the gift you really want!

103. Speak only kindly. Keep going.

104. Wrap yourself in warm towels from the dryer after your bath.

105. Unschedule. Make room for magic!

106. Invite someone special to breakfast.

107. Do holiday zentangles with the kids.

108. Take holiday photos of your pets in their holiday outfits!

109. Wear Christmas sweaters, holiday pjs, or funny holiday hats and take a fun family photo.

110. Remove things from your to-do list.

111. Snuggle up under soft, cozy blankets on the couch for a family movie marathon. Watch all of a TV Series or Movie Franchise.

112. Give yourself permission to say "no."

113.   Enjoy hot cocoa, spiced mulled cider, or a pumpkin spiced latte.

114.   Make a list of every good thing you, or you and your partner, or you and your family did this past year. Give thanks for the great memories!

115.   Take family walks to de-stress. Walk off the passive-aggressive family members' comments. Walk off the close quarters, the shot nerves, and the political tension. Keep walking.

116.   Go get a festive manicure and/or pedicure with your besties. Will you choose cherry red, evergreen, or winter white holiday sparkle?

117.   Journal about everything you are already grateful for.

118.   Listen to classic holiday favorites (Johnny Cash, Elvis, Aretha Franklin, Tony Bennett, or Frank Sinatra.) Slow dance in the kitchen.

119.   Recreate a cherished childhood memory today. Set up a train set, play in the dollhouse, or make your Nona's cookies. Reminisce.

120.   Let yourself really enjoy the holiday food without feeling guilty or beating yourself up. Ditch the calorie talk. Ditch the diet talk. Give that gift to yourself, and everyone around you.

121.   Color in your holiday coloring book, in your holiday pjs, by the fire.

122.   Have a sleepover under the Christmas tree!

123.   Call an old friend and wish them a Happy Hanukkah, a Merry Christmas, or a Happy New Year! Tell them how much you love them and miss them. Reconnect.

124.   Get the whole family some kooky holiday socks to stay

warm and toasty.

125.   Make it a pajama day.

126.   Make relaxing a priority.

127.   Make a special holiday treat with the kids. Make Rice
         Krispie treats, a Yule log, latkes, Christmas fudge, or
         peppermint brownies.

128.   Go on a holiday photo walk with the kids, or with your
         friends.

129.   Take yourself out for a holiday treat. Go get a special
         dessert. Order a fancy coffee. Have a beautiful pastry.
         Enjoy!

130.   Go caroling!

131.   Do a body scan. What does your body need?

132.   Order pizza.

133.   Read the kids holiday books before bed every night in December.

134.   Actually schedule your downtime in your planner and on your calendar.

135.   Go get a haircut! Feel fresh for the brand new year. Coco Chanel once said, "A woman who cuts her hair is about to change her life! "

136.   Ask for help. Hire out. Delegate tasks.

137.   Go see a holiday play. Go sing The Messiah. Or go to a holiday sing-a-long.

138.   Lower your expectations.

139.   Write about your holiday memories in your journal.

140.   Play "Elf on the Shelf." You can do it for the kids. Let the older teens help you.

141.   Take your vitamins.

142.   Eat some fruit.

143.   Make fresh juice.

144.   Give your whole body a good smelling sugar scrub.

145.   Drink more water.

146.   Go see a movie matinee by yourself.

147.   Skip the holiday cards and send Valentines in a few months, instead.

148.   Make handmade holiday cards for some of your list, not the whole list.

149.   Light holiday candles in seasonal scents like pumpkin pie, cinnamon apple, wintergreen, pine, sugar cookie, gingerbread, or toasted marshmallow.

150.   Go take a drive together to look at the holiday lights and the festive decorations. It is free, and very hygge!

Made in the USA
San Bernardino,
CA